Wind

Look for the other books on weather by

Marion Dane Bauer
Snow • Rain • Clouds
Rainbow • Sun

Simon Spotlight
An imprint of Simon & Schuster Children's Publishing Division
1230 Avenue of the Americas, New York, NY 10020
This Simon Spotlight edition May 2016
First Simon Spotlight edition November 2011
First Aladdin edition September 2003
Text copyright © 2003 by Marion Dane Bauer
Illustrations copyright © 2003 by John Wallace
For information about special discounts for bulk purchases, please contact
Simon & Schuster Special Sales at 1-866-506-1949
or business@simonandschuster.com.
Book design by Debra Sfetsios
The text of this book was set in Century Schoolbook.
Manufactured in the United States of America 0416 LAK
2 4 6 8 10 9 7 5 3 1
Library of Congress Cataloging-in-Publication Data
Bauer, Marion Dane.
Wind / Marion Dane Bauer ; illustrated by John Wallace.— 1st Aladdin
Paperbacks ed.
p. cm. — (Ready-to-read)
Summary: Illustrations and simple text explain what wind is, how it is
used by plants, birds, and people, and how wind can become a storm.
1. Winds—Juvenile literature. [1. Winds.] I. Wallace, John, 1966–
ill. II. Title. III. Series.
QC931.4.B38 2004
551.51'8—dc21
2002009656
ISBN 978-1-4814-6215-0 (hc)
ISBN 978-0-689-85443-9 (pbk)
ISBN 978-1-4424-9049-4 (eBook)

Wind

written by Marion Dane Bauer

illustrated by John Wallace

Ready-to-Read

Simon Spotlight
New York London Toronto Sydney New Delhi

The earth we live on
is a spinning ball.

When the earth spins,
the air around it
moves too.

When air moves,
we call it "wind."
As the sun heats the air,
the air grows lighter.
Light air rises.

Cool air is heavy.
It falls.

Cool air and warm air
are always trading places.

We call this movement "wind."

Birds use wind
to help them fly.

Plants use wind
to carry their seeds.

We use wind
to fly kites,

to sail boats,

and to turn
windmills.

Wind moves clouds.

Wind makes waves.

It even makes trees bend.

When the hot air
is very light
and the cold air
is very heavy,
wind can blow up a storm!

Sometimes wind spins
like a puppy
chasing its tail.

A small spin
makes a dust devil
or a water spout.

A strong spin
makes a tornado
or a hurricane.

Wind can be scary.

Or it can sing
a gentle song.

Wind is all around us,
but we cannot see it.

We can only see
what wind does.

Facts about wind:

The air that surrounds the Earth is called the troposphere. It is only about eight miles deep.

The hardest gust of wind ever measured was on Mount Washington. It was 231 miles per hour.

When wind blows snow very hard, we have a blizzard.

The eye of a hurricane is still. The winds are quiet there. After the eye passes, the winds blow in the opposite direction.